CAPACITY

Radical but Persuasive Godly Perspectives

JOAN JONES

Author of *The Low Sodium Diet:*
Stop Agonizing by Embracing a Low Salt Life

ISBN 978-1-63903-299-0 (paperback)
ISBN 978-1-63903-300-3 (digital)

Christian Faith Publishing, Inc.
832 Park Avenue
Meadville, PA 16335
www.christianfaithpublishing.com

Printed in the United States of America

To our delightful son, Kris, who always brings great joy to our lives. His dedication to God, family, and friends is amazing.

Contents

Our Ideals Hinge on These Two Words

Does a person *undoubtedly* know whether he has the *capacity* or the *ability* to achieve anything he's ever imagined? Astounding findings cause us to take a second look at the possibilities.

Stimulating life stories, in-depth research, and other examples from a biblical standpoint will illuminate our minds to the true meaning of these two words, and we'll see why they are *not identical*. We'll also see how God's plan can take us to the summit of our aspirations.

We can *flourish* in every category of our lives based on the simple understanding of our *capacity* versus our *ability*, as we exert every effort to become the champions God wants us to be. When we *withhold* nothing, we're *able* to claim the things that mean the most to us. As we let go of inhibitions or fears, we're finally free to explore, *thrive,* and bask in the sunshine of a life that is vibrant and abundant!

> According as His divine power has given unto us all things that pertain unto life and godliness, through the knowledge of Him that has called us to glory and virtue. (2 Peter 1:3 KJV)

Withholding our very best

Our greatest successes in life are realized when we refuse to *withhold,* fully sharing our talents and genius with the world. We were born to serve; it benefits us and the recipients.

> Give and it shall be given unto you; good measure, pressed down, and shaken together, and

running over, shall men give into your bosom. For with the same measure that ye mete withal it shall be measured to you again. (Luke 6:38 KJV)

Increase in Love Capacity?

Can we increase our capacity to love? This subject is a relatively delicate one and worthy of scrutiny. It is close to the heart of many, and why not? *God is love.* Virtually the whole world is affected in one way or another by love or lack of it—truly an understatement!

Love is the nucleus of life, *created by God*, who spoke everything into existence—both great and small.

> God in the beginning created the heaven and the earth. (Genesis 1:1 KJV)

Concerned about her husband's *capacity* to love, one lady confided in me. It's instantly recognizable from his social lifestyle and devotion to his family that he doesn't have the *slightest* romantic interest in *anyone else* but his wife—proven over their several years of marriage. Yet she's sometimes uneasy about his composure and lack of outward show of passion. That's just his style. Yet she maintains he has an *apparent strong capacity* to love her—one fortunate lady!

Many people endure insecurities of this nature; no gender is spared.

Frequency of communication

It appears that the *capacity to love* can be innocently infringed upon by demands for more attentiveness by a spouse or anyone else whose demands are unreasonable. But since there's no way to assess love other than by *actions*, we're usually at a loss to know its *intensity.* So *for this reason*, love is still questioned. The only alternative we have is to love unconditionally and leave the rest in the hands of the *only* reliable source we know—God Almighty, who is the judge of all.

Frequent communication between you and your spouse cannot be overstressed. It is the *lifeblood* of a good marriage. This is one area where we can be tricked by the adversary, the enemy of our lives. One of his schemes, *often in subtle ways*, is to destroy marriages. We have to be diligent to enforce ways of keeping them fresh and captivating. We're aware of the failures that often come from a lack of communication.

> Lest Satan should get an advantage of us: for we are not ignorant of his devices. (2 Corinthians 2:11 KJV)

Embrace every moment together

Many of us have jobs where we're glued to our desks or computers for at least eight hours each day. That's one deterrent to frequent communication and understandably so. What a major reason for us to embrace every moment when we can be together, to relax and reconnect after a tedious day away from each other. We can also make adjustments when the hours we work vary.

When we put *God first* in our lives, he directs our steps to live a life that is more vibrant and abundant, which includes a fulfilled and happy marriage.

The nucleus of life

It would be trivial to undertake exploring all aspects of love, but in an attempt to be exhaustive, some are worth delving into. These truths regarding love are inspiring:

- God *is* love
- True love never fails—is unconditional

- It is unselfish, not envious
- Love is tolerant of others
- It is kind; doesn't think evil (doesn't keep a record of evil done)
- Is not boastful
- Doesn't celebrate the ruin of others (does not rejoice in iniquity)

These attributes can be found in the Bible in 1 Corinthians 13.

It would be negligent to avoid mentioning different types of love since each *emotion* of love differs one from another. Clearly, all love is *not the same*. But make no mistake, *love is love*; it is always good and does only good. For example, *take a look at babies* how they obviously express what we clearly recognize as love, how they endear themselves to us.

The love of God as expressed above is unconditional and is the Greek word *agape*, which is "the love of God in the *renewed mind* in manifestation." It is just not possible to love the unlovely without *agape* love. Only God has the explanation for this, yet the phenomenon is genuine. Individuals born of the spirit of God, who have invited Jesus Christ into their lives and believe God raised him from the dead, have the ability to practice *agape* love.

The love I felt for my father is *absolutely not* the same that I feel for my husband. The contrast most would agree is noteworthy. That *instantly* reminds us that the emotions we experience when we love are distinctly diverse. Similarly, the love I felt for my baby boy cannot be compared in any sense to what I feel for another person regardless of association or age.

Eros is romantic, sexual, or intimate love. *Philia* (from where we get the word Philadelphia, City of Brotherly Love) is that deep friendship and love that exists among people in general, old friends and acquaintances.

Loving ourselves

There's something extraordinarily liberating about this! No, we're not inferring narcissism. On the contrary, we believe that *most* people were born with the *capacity* to love not only themselves but others as well. Some have suggested that this love of self may even be a deterrent to loneliness.

There are multiple reasons why a person does not have the *capacity* to love himself or herself. Any or all of the following may apply:

- They've been deprived of a healthy family life.
- Negative circumstances caused them to have a low self-esteem.
- They may have been mistreated by individuals in authority.
- They've been adopted and there was rivalry among siblings.

This list is not exhaustive. The answer to any of these is by accepting the support of a loving and caring father—God Almighty, the Creator of all of us, who understands all things that pertain to *every aspect* of our lives. We all have the option to start afresh. Though it may not be easy it sure beats the alternative.

(Relevant link: www.positivepsychologynews.com)

Our Capacity to Concede

I don't know of anyone who lives under a rock; we are not unaware or ignorant of the devastations that seem to be present in our world. *Most of us* would agree there's an opposing force that comes against us, endeavoring to make our lives miserable and gloomy. *This is not the will of God*, our Creator. *His will is for our safety and happiness.*

Principalities, powers, and rulers of darkness monopolize the system of orderliness and the good life that is *God's intent* for everyone. His *capacity and ability* to be all sufficient exceed our complexities. He has *all* the answers we need when we trust in him and cleave to his reliable Word. So there's no reason to concede to our adversary. As a matter of *truth,* he was *defeated* when Jesus Christ died on the cross, paying the ransom that brought us back to God. So as Christians the adversary has *absolutely no grip on us.*

Accurate and dependable resource

There is a *fascinating resource* that millions turn to. The Bible is the guaranteed Word of God. It is his will for humanity. And according to the *Guinness Book of World Records,* it remains *the* number one best-selling, nonfiction book in the world—over *five billion* copies sold! So there has to be solid, plausible reasons for this astonishing evidence.

The Bible is a *game-changer* for the following reasons:

- Reliance on its principles is rewarding when appropriated.
- We have the *capacity* to acknowledge it as truth.
- It contains everything that pertains to life and godliness.

- It's strikingly engaging. We question why more movies aren't produced based on the numerous mind-boggling stories that have been recorded!
- Even though many versions are available and contested, its *core message* is upheld.
- When we claim it as our own, it delivers the same results that it did thousands of years ago.
- Its emphasis is clear—*we have a savior who lived, died, and rose again* to redeem mankind and fulfill the will of God, his Father.

Relevant links

www.guinnessworldrecords.com
www.jamesclear.com

Capacity to Effectively Communicate

The conduct that we sometimes flaunt during conversation isn't always our preference since we do care about others! But many of us have trespassed in some way. We have the *ability* to generate stimulating conversation. There is always an overabundance of ideas about which we can exchange our opinions. Knowing how to make it a win for both parties takes focus and courteousness.

Paying attention to a person while talking to them is not only vital but demonstrates respect for someone who might desperately crave our opinion. So glancing over at someone else or playing with our phone while conversing can be distracting—*news flash!*

Examples to emulate

Envision how listening to the opinions and feelings of one another invokes harmony, a sense of camaraderie, and display of compassion. Imagine yourself as the recipient! What a decent and noble way to conduct ourselves.

We can follow in the steps of Jesus Christ, whose kindness and love for people excelled that of any other human being. He was perfect but left us examples to emulate so that we can grow in that area of our lives. It's all about growth; we don't want to merely exist or remain stagnant. The more we practice the faster our progress becomes.

The use of acronyms, jargon, slangs

It may be complicated to convey our meanings when language is replete with acronyms, slangs, or jargon that may only be related to us or our career and interests. Straightforwardness and clarity can be the substance for channeling the exchange of our thoughts.

Eye-to-eye contact

When someone initiates a question, it's reasonable to direct our thoughts to that person and give them the respect of an eye-to-eye contact instead of to another person present whom we may favor better. It may be one way the *capacity* to discipline one's mind is tested since it's not always the easiest thing to do. But the exchange of words becomes friendlier and time spent together is worthwhile.

Bond with empathy

What *if only* we could vicariously during conversation enter the lives and worlds of those people with whom we're connecting? What a privilege that would be! People in general don't have the *capacity* for being directly or indirectly dictated to but rather often value sound advice when solicited. We have the *ability* to reach people's hearts when they have our undivided attention. Using discretion is challenging when conversing because we naturally want the sound of our voice to be cohesive, persuasive, and not leave room for confusion in the mind of the listener.

Facial expressions send glaring messages

Listening three quarters of the time without interruption doesn't seem like a natural option for most of us during a conversation. To some, the thought might be considered peculiar, but specialists concur that this actually works. It is a key quality to possess when someone is desirous of our receptiveness.

This doesn't only take *ability* but willingness to meet the needs of others. It would seem like the *capacity* to listen isn't as *demanding* as in other areas like these:

- The *capacity* to control anger
- To be selfless
- To embrace solitude
- To endure listening to gossip

The pleasant tone of your voice, your eye contact, and your facial expressions send strong messages to the other person and may ease tensions during a dialogue.

> Wherefore, my beloved brethren, let every-
> one be swift to hear, slow to speak, slow to wrath.
> (James 1:19 KJV)

(Relevant link: www.habitsforwellbeing.com)

Capacity as a Stay-at-Home Mom

My mom really didn't have a choice; my parents had twelve children (six boys and six girls, whom she'd often jokingly call *the twelve tribes*). However, she had the *capacity*, and I must add ability to totally enjoy being at home with us. This experience could be claustrophobic for some moms, but she was *one in millions*.

One terrifying day, my three-year-old brother got into mischief. He thought it'd be a cool idea to shove the chalk he was playing with into his nostrils. Although chalk is mostly calcium carbonate and nontoxic, he knew no better and was traumatized.

Mama, who in spite of her various duties had the *capacity* to remain calm, promptly got in touch with our cousin Joyce, an RN, who soon came to his rescue.

Restricted by their capacities

Women are spending time at home with their children, relinquishing the hustle and commotion of venturing into the business environment. They feel entangled and pushed beyond their *capacity*. Although most of these women may have the *ability* to care for their children at home, their emotional *capacities* differ and are *undeniable*. Our unwavering support and understanding can be shown in these situations, recognizing that we too have foibles in ways that are inexplicable.

Naturally, there are advantages and disadvantages to being a stay-at-home mom. Mothers have the freedom to choose wisely what best suits their lifestyle.

Benefits or hazards related to choices

Here's a list that might be of interest to us before our final decisions are locked in. We always want to know what might be the most satisfying and rewarding for us and our children.

- It is quite common that anxiety accompanies the *inability* to cope as stay-at-home moms. It may also lead to dire mental, emotional, or physical maladies. A *professional therapist or counselor* may be contacted for support in these instances to help restore wholeness, energy, and enjoyment of life.

- One major advantage of being a mother at home is being able to train children during those formative years by teaching them the Bible while they're still *bendable* and responsive to this invaluable resource. The greatness of it is the *benchmark* for all other instructions as we live this new and exciting life! Seeing positive results in our child's behavior is a triumph that parents can rest in and fully appreciate.

- Statistics show that seventy-one percent of women now work outside of the home, and the percentage is rapidly rising; twenty-nine percent stay at home. One of the many reasons for the change is the fact that women have become more independent economically, educationally, and socially.

- Some studies have shown that school performance is enhanced in both older and younger children whose parents are at home but was significantly higher with the younger group.

- The *National Home Education Institute* provides statistics validating success in children whose parent provides education at home. It was also proven that those children gained fifteen to thirty percentile points higher than others.

- While in the comfort of our homes, meeting deadlines is virtually unnecessary. For example, those encountered when working in an office can be unsettling. Instead, the flow of work in our home can be adapted to suit momentary demands, as compared to running on a boss' time crunch.

- *The National Institute of Child Health and Human Development* and the *Institute of Child Development* of the *University of Minnesota* further reveal that children in day care centers display more stress and aggressive behavior than those who are trained at home. Their subsequent findings from follow-up research concurred with original findings approximately seven years earlier.
- *Here's the best part*: there are many other options available for stay-at-home moms to get the social breaks they need whenever necessary. Their children can have connections and develop friendships with other children by visiting parks, recreation centers, or in the homes of other parents who also train from home, to name just a few. With so many resources available, we can find ways to teach and entertain our kids.

A Gallup poll of sixty thousand mothers included:

- Women with no children
- Working moms
- Stay-at-home moms

It was suggested that stay-at-home moms faced the most anxiety, sadness, or anger.

Notably, according to *Pew Research Center*'s social and demographic trend, sixty percent of Americans claim having a parent at home is priceless; thirty-five percent claim that children are just as well off with both parents working away from the home.

Train up a child in the way he should go
and when he is old, he will not depart from it.
(Proverbs 22:6 KJV)

This implies that children have the *capacity* to receive right teaching. The *ability to retain* what's being taught may differ from child to child, based on their surroundings, upbringing, or other restrictions.

Relevant links

www.amotherfarfromhome.com
www.verywellfamily.com

Observing Capacity from a Legal Perception

A legal viewpoint suggests that the word "capacity" implies competence when making day-today choices that influence one's life. These choices may relate to some of the following:

- The moment a doctor should be seen; the choice of a doctor
- Judgments regarding legal matters
- Purchasing decisions
- The best place to live
- Financial considerations
- Services and assistance needed

People who live independently and are able to understand, consider, and communicate what the outcome of their decisions might be are regarded as having the *capacity*. Otherwise, having a substitute may be compulsory to assist in making these decisions, especially when it involves matters like preparing tax returns.

Making choices of a more personal nature—like purchasing clothing, deciding which restaurant is best, or when to exercise—may be second nature to someone who is otherwise dependent.

Regarding emotional and physical well-being

We cannot generalize or pinpoint the *capacity* from one individual to another as circumstances differ just as much as people. Much thought is given to a person relative to their emotional or physical well-being and whether or not they receive services of any kind.

Additionally, people are affected by their surroundings, so that *capacity* is unpredictable and *immeasurable*. For example, living in a dilapidated home under disturbing conditions may stunt a healthy emotional and physical growth for some. Others under the same disorders may be entirely unaffected.

Interestingly, the extent of someone's *capacity* may depend on issues like the following:

- Decisions being made—is it financial or personal?
- Are the decisions simple or complex?
- How information is given and the degree to which it is assimilated and understood
- Successful communication among individuals

When in doubt, connecting with authorized health professionals such as doctors, psychologists, social workers, occupational therapists, or nurses is advisable to determine the extent of one's ability or readiness to change.

Relevant links

www.justice.nsw.gov
www.nsbs.org
www.sciencedirect.com

Capacity Coping with Big Crowds

Overpowering is the term used for the sensation some people feel when they find themselves in huge crowds! Their *capacity* in such situations doesn't allow them the freedom to break loose and become involved in the celebrations of the moment. Quite frankly, for them, it's not even worth contemplating since that may imply that they just might be expected to participate. So they dismiss the thought at the onset and retreat back into their comfort zone.

Some people suffer from a disorder called post-traumatic stress disorder (PTSD), which is triggered by being in large crowds, especially when living in a city where street celebrations are the norm. Others simply dislike being in large crowds. For PTSD sufferers, the feeling is like being trapped, which stirs up anxiety and fear. These moods can discourage you from leaving your home.

Bring along a companion

It's wise to always have a friend along for support and advice in these situations. If they're not aware of your anxieties, it would be a great idea to discuss with them upfront the things that might spark panic or any uneasiness.

Plan the length of time you want to be in a certain crowded location and try not to exceed the time you specified. The longer you stick around, the more likely you are to have attacks.

Relax by practicing *deep breathing* to alleviate anxiety and stress that accompany PTSD. It is a quick go-to solution when you feel stuck and are unable to quickly find a way out of your environment.

Identify easily accessible locations

Here are a few eye-openers:

- Identifying the triggers of PTSD is essential. You don't want to isolate yourself or miss out on some of the pleasures of living by being unaware when an attack might strike.
- Be aware of your surroundings. One great strategy is to know the location of easily accessible areas, so when necessary, you can escape the masses.
- Always *connect with your doctor* for advice and information concerning all of your health needs. Your health care provider is one of your best friends. We cannot completely avoid being around crowds, but there's a lot we can do to ease the panic and enjoy being a part of the action.

On a personal note, the Fourth of July is a holiday I look forward to. The downtown celebrations in the city where I live are worth savoring. I have this innate *capacity* to enjoy seeing crowds of thousands present during this momentous event. There's just something enchanting about seeing the faces of various nationalities, especially on a bright and sunny July day.

Although people who avoid crowds may have the *ability* to participate, there's something that causes them to *withdraw* from *extending* themselves beyond what others might find necessary and comfortable. Generally, we don't know why that is, but if it becomes overwhelming to the point of causing severe discomfort or sickness, then a cautious step would be to *connect with a health care professional for consultation.*

The other's shoes

It would be a *harsh conclusion* to assume that individuals under these conditions are selfish or introverted. Sometimes it's a good idea to take a step back, reason, and merely aim to assume ourselves in the other person's shoes. This benefits them and us; we have an occasion to assess ourselves, which in turn takes the pressure off them.

My little children, let us not love in word, neither in tongue; but indeed and in truth. (1 John 3:18 KJV)

Relevant links

www.quora.com
www.verywellmind.com

A Daring Experiment

Humorous enough to envision! If the *can* holds *only* three grams, then it'd be a far-fetched notion *struggling* to cram anymore into it. An eccentric person *might* attempt the feat, hoping that for some strange reason it "just might work."

Some might think this effort *peculiar*, but for others, it could be just a *bold experiment* to discover *something new* by attempting this impossible, unproductive task. But seriously, it's amazing how thoughts can spring from different directions bestowing on us some mild entertainment.

The boundaries of common sense

Interesting discoveries of the use of the words "capacity" and "ability" in my personal life and the lives of others with whom I'm acquainted led me to further inquiries. It was not surprising to find how many categories exist. By accepting the following *promise* of God, we can live within the boundaries of common sense.

> I will instruct thee and teach thee in the way
> which thou shall go: I will guide thee with my
> eye. (Psalm 32:8 KJV)

As we embrace him, God guides us in our decisions based on the integrity of his Word. Doing less may lead us in paths that are worthless, depriving us of the best life he has to offer.

Ability to do, understand, or experience

It doesn't matter how lofty our achievements, we all have *something* that we admit is far beyond our reach, something that we have given up. Even worse, we've never tried but have surrendered to the notion that it *may* never be attained. We're content to relinquish the whole idea. So in exchange, we enjoy comfort in knowing that everything else we've done and experienced *reasonably* compensates. *Why not?*

Prevalent thoughts of uncertainty

We may think that fulfilling our dream is "way above our heads" either *to understand or do*. No one can *honestly* claim perfection in every aspect of life. The people we often emulate have struggles of their own. So giving up on a dream shouldn't be an option; we might want to first give it our all.

Imagine if we never tried to accomplish the one thing we've always wanted but hold on to our *thoughts of uncertainty*! Quite often, the possibility of succeeding is certain after we've taken that first step. And how we often surprise ourselves as we take the second and third and then become unstoppable.

Not unqualified by competition

It can be almost unbearable observing how adept others are, doing or experiencing the things we've always craved; this merely nurtures our fears of never reaching the pinnacle of our expectations. We assume that we're unqualified in the competition (by which everything is unfairly judged). We might decide to *chuck* the idea of aspiring to do whatever "that" might be. God has given us the *capacity* to entertain godly desires, which he gives to us. These desires enrich our lives so we can learn, grow, and be able to reach and teach others in the way that will bring them deliverance and freedom.

> Delight thyself in the Lord; and He shall give thee the desires of thine heart. (Psalm 37:4 KJV)

Ability versus Capacity to Follow Through

A highly qualified auto mechanic with a sterling business record may have the *ability* to recover the damage of multiple cars; however, much depends on his *capacity* to process the receipt of numerous requests for his service. He *undoubtedly* can do the work but may have this underlying sense of "*limitation.*" This sometimes tends to creep into the mind, forcing us to *draw the line*; being convinced that "the line" is where we need to discontinue the task.

Allow ourselves to soar to safe heights

This is the time to rely on *the highest power,* God, to stimulate and awaken our very best selves in taking further action. We'll realize we have the *capacity* for much more than we give ourselves credit for. We can soar as far as we allow ourselves by trusting that what God says about us is true. He left no stone unturned by repeatedly stressing in his Word how capable, strong, and victorious we can be.

> I can do all things through Christ which strengthens me. (Philippians 4:13)

How refreshing to know that we can fulfill our heartfelt desires to *follow through* till the end, undisturbed by our false ideas or that of others around us. We can be well on the way to realizing our victories.

Nurturing in the home

Time spent in school from a very young age brings out the very best or worst in most of us. Much, of course, depends on our influences in the home—the nucleus of learning. My *capacity* to learn to write early in life was further heightened by my parents' probing. I wrote on everything, from the walls in our home to the desks at school and other easily accessible places. I used every imaginable writing implement I could find to satisfy my interest.

Exercising our aptitudes and proficiencies allows us to ascend to the top. Without our display of effort, we'd more than likely require much training and determination to reach reasonable goals. Teachers engender and foster the atmosphere necessary for the growth of students, but overall *nurturing begins in the home*, especially where the truth of God's Word is taught and godly examples are emulated.

Relevant links

www.psychologydictionary.com
www.britannica.com

Capacity for Civic Involvement

Although the major factors that embody *capacity* for civic *involvement* might be *enthusiasm* and *zeal*, the *skills* for properly perceiving and distinguishing facts may not be present. Making firm, bold judgments that are relevant in a community, neighborhood, or nation requires ample reasoning to attain a satisfactory conclusions based on fairness to solve the problem being addressed.

If a civic group lacks the *ability* to act and think collectively as result of the lack of sufficient resources or exclusion from participation in decision-making activities, grassroots citizens are genuinely rendered immobilized.

Grassroots inclusion in decision-making

Frustration among grassroots citizens that believe they're excluded from the mainstream decision-making processes sometimes leads to disorder and chaos in a community. It may be needful for officials and representatives to take the necessary stand to enforce inclusion of grassroots civilians at civic events.

A well organized and guarded event could accommodate eager attendees who will contribute positively to the agenda by imparting their knowledge of current events and providing solutions. These can be researched and enforced to implement new beginnings and move forward with established regulations and policies that benefit the community.

Regulations and policies that aren't beneficial to the general community are standards that are lacking in substance and are unjust. Jesus Christ, who is the supreme example of justice, taught principles to live by as recorded in God's Word. When these are fully grasped and followed, the results are *phenomenal*. We have the *ability* as Christians to become involved in improving the life of our communities by injecting standards that are an asset to God, ourselves, and others.

Political scientists launched an eleven-city study of school reform in 1993, centering on the awareness of civic *capacity*. Those with low levels of civic *capacity* never focused on concerns that mattered to those of higher levels but were sporadic and not concerted in their efforts. Those of a higher-level *capacity* came together in a rigorous attempt to improve their communities. An established leadership base that includes both grassroots and elites should be implemented to solve problems and disputes with fairness.

Relevant links

www.journals.sagepub.com
www.newamerica.org

Memory Capacity of the Human Brain

The mere thought of this amazing discovery that the brain just may be able to contain the entire Internet is mind-boggling. It is calculated that the brain has the *capacity* to store a quadrillion bytes of data and that it has more efficiency than a computer. We never have to worry about running out of *brain capacity* during our lifespan. This query is not new; scholars have probed the brain's *capacity*. It's difficult to compute its memory storage. Another amazing scientific finding validates the reality that our brain storage is astonishing; it can store over four billion books—staggering!

According to *Clinical Neurology Specialists*, the brain can store trillions of bytes of information. Storage of the brain is limited to about one megabyte daily. So far, there is no record of anyone reaching that limit, so we can only speculate at best.

Incredible estimated memory

Other scientists deny the finding (which is considered a myth) that humans use only ten percent of the brain, reasoning that information can be stored in every segment of the brain. Salk researchers have discovered that the human brain has a higher memory *capacity* than was originally estimated.

> I will praise thee; for I am fearfully [lit., awesomely], and wonderfully made. Marvelous are thy works; and that my soul knows right well. Psalm 139:14 KJV)

Relevant links

www.scientificamerica.com
www.clinicalneurologyspecialist.com
www.telegraph.co.uk
www.slate.com
www.futurism.com

Having Innate Capacity

This may be a good inheritance or a bad one. Innate *capacity* is present from the time one is born. This may be a *benefit* (or not) that's passed down to progenies and bypasses new learning or experience. For instance, math for a family member of mine was as easy as *breathing*; it would have been unreasonable to deny the reality. Yet for the rest of us, it could be described as *gasping for breath* (maybe not quite that bad). But having him around was an asset, someone we could turn to.

I think about how I've always liked math and my performance was fair, but it never surpassed his. My *capacity* seemed to be restricted. A rational thought is that I probably could have achieved comparable results had I been *willing* to work harder and *extend* my efforts.

By the way, I discovered that the energy that was put forth into learning math was rewarding and spare me embarrassment when shopping, deciphering the accuracy of tax return statements, or knowing that the records in my bank account are spot-on. Can't think of any other reasons why I'd want to be a math wizard.

A natural knack

Some scientific experiments have shown that an innate *capacity* for math is something that many people possess. Even though other scientists have argued otherwise, it remains inexplicable. It seems that the brain is preprogrammed, allowing it to gain intelligence that's beyond what we can envision.

Relevant links

www.quora.com
www.scienceclarified.com

Immeasurable Capacity in Human Greatness

No one will ever know the enormity of the human mind—the *capacity* to achieve ultimate greatness. What is *ultimate* greatness anyway? Has any one person ever really achieved this? Where is the line drawn? Someone once said to me, "I'm not always right, but I'm never wrong." It's a hard pill to swallow, but *most* people admit that none of us is perfect.

We can develop our capacities to be even greater. This leads us to pursue excellence in a way that is pleasantly impacting. While being our true selves, we can be involved in competition that is challenging and persuades us to be right where we want to be. If we're great at what we do, we're sure to be an inspiration to others, something we should be proud of.

Born to win in the competition of life

For most of us, the possibilities are endless when our determination, capacities, and abilities are strong. When playing any sport, we choose a team whose goals are to move forward with tenacity, people who do not submit easily to the opponent; winning is their aim, and playing a fair game to them is paramount.

We're born to win, and God is our coach; he directs our steps as we walk in his ways. His will is that we're never ashamed or embarrassed with our performance, so we expend every ounce of strength in order to win. Whenever we choose to do our part *regardless of what others are doing*, we become formidable.

The world looks on at our *hard-nosed* approach and the way we focus to arrive at our destiny. This is what's vital to becoming excellent in whatever we choose to do. The recompense is incomparable and well worth the effort and time.

Solid commitment to goals

As we set goals we strive with passion to tirelessly pursue them to the finish line. That's the reason why *doing what we love* is essential. It's futile to set goals that may not be accomplished because of a lack of desire and commitment to the goal. We may be interested in something yet not possess a strong desire to participate in it.

Procrastination is never the place we want to inhabit; it is an unhealthy habit to adopt; it has been the cause of many lost opportunities, among other things. And in some cases, once these opportunities are gone, there's no way to recovery. Also, it's reckless to grab every seeming opportunity since it's not always clear to us what is and what's not. Guidance from God is the way to go! He really *is able* to guide us so that we don't (out of desperation) *trip* into unwanted pitfalls that may be in the guise of "opportunities."

Relevant links

www.huffingtonpost.com
www.coachville.com
https://link.springer.com

Capacity for Physical Exercise

Exercise *capacity* is limited by what can be tolerated. To establish a conclusion of precise evaluation of exercise capacity, it is imperative that exertion be adequately prolonged. When energy is persistent and consistent, *capacity* can be determined. We want to always listen to our bodies. Our muscles depend upon oxygen and substrates of carbohydrates during exercise, so pumping up our consumption of oxygen only benefits us.

By *developing* our *capacity* for aerobics, our bodies easily adapt to effectively using oxygen. Another compelling advantage for developing our aerobic *capacity* is that it can enhance the flow of our oxygenated blood to muscle tissue. Dancing too can help to develop our aerobic *capacity*. What a pleasurable way to see expected results. Classes are everywhere we look; it's almost like being at a party with friends while enhancing your capacity!

Exercise capacity in kids

Children may already be doing the *Physical Activity Guidelines for Americans* of sixty minutes daily, as suggested by the Center for Disease Control and Prevention (CDC), by participating in aerobics, muscle strengthening, and bone strengthening activities at school. They have the inherent *capacity* to be sustained throughout this period.

According to health practitioners, exercise intolerance varies from child to child and can be caused by a loss of strength and stamina resulting from malnutrition or other health problems like asthma, breathing or heart problems.

Relevant links

www.nationaljewish.org
www.cdc.com
https://www.cdc.gov
www.ncbi.nlm.nih.gov
www.acefitness.com

The Capacity for Awareness

We are persuaded to *be in tune with* our heavenly Father so that we're not oblivious when our well-being is challenged by forces that are contrary to his will for our lives. We have the *ability* to be steadfast, not in our strength but by his *incomparable power*, love, and care for us.

As we decide not to conform to the dictates and subtleties of this world, we can determine what his will is for us. What an *exceptionally extraordinary life* this is, knowing that we have someone we can *actually* rely on twenty-four seven!

> And be not conformed to this world: but be
> transformed by the renewing of your mind that
> ye may prove what is that good, and acceptable,
> and perfect will of God. (Romans 12:2 KJV)

The radical change

Just telling people to renew their minds is not as effective as showing them *how they can* from the Bible. This is obviously not always easy, especially when one has never had a *change in heart*, which comes by accepting Jesus Christ as personal Lord and Savior, believing that God raised him from the dead and starting a new life. Then *in that instant*, a loving God begins to guide us *step-by-step*.

This is the first stage to having a renewed mind and beginning an adventure of freedom and deliverance, which enables us to see the truths presented in his Word. Then we're no longer spiritually blinded. Even when we've become Christians, it takes being patient with ourselves, giving God a chance to work in and through us. It's a moment by moment walk with him. This is a personal decision that people around the world make daily and experience indisputable success based on the principles found in the Bible.

Our Genuine Capacity to Cope

It's astonishing that we have this natural passion and ability to adapt and transform situations that sometimes seem to be beyond our control. We extend our strengths in assisting our fellow men to protect ourselves and them when needs arise. We use our resources and well-acquired skills to lighten one another's burdens in times of adversities and other difficult circumstances.

In the aftermath of disasters, the true test of our ability to cope and unite is apparent. We always seem to have this *capacity* to pool our resources and advance with the dignity, pride, and care for one another that hold us all together as human entities.

Surpassing our understanding

Our regard for God plays an inevitable part in our desire to become involved in serving others and being a part of *a larger family* than those in our individual households. When challenged we cope in ways *beyond our own understanding* and extend all of ourselves, withholding nothing that is valuable in our quest to live united and free, we adapt to changes and manage successfully together during crises.

Our capacity to unselfishly serve

There is no room for selfish desires during trying times. Somehow, by not *withholding* our abilities but willingly reaching out to others seems to be innate in most people, there's that desire to give part of ourselves, knowing our lives will be enriched, and we will have learned much about the needs of our fellow men and about our true selves. We grow in our knowledge of one another.

Serving is a unique opportunity to express our true selves, an occasion to reach beyond what we believe we can do to satisfy the needs of others. We always seem to get rewarded, especially when we serve without expectation of being reciprocated.

> Behold, how good and how pleasant it is for
> brethren to dwell together in unity! (Psalm 133:1
> KJV)

(Relevant link: www.environment.gov)

Capacity to Contain Oneself

Imagine being stuck in a tightly fitting barrel! It's pretty difficult to move around. Losing control of our emotions is *somewhat* comparable but it is a pressure we allow, forcing us to be as equally restricted!

Too funny to stop

At times, when someone tells an amazingly funny story, it's almost impossible to contain myself; my *capacity* to laugh is a hearty one, and I'm inclined to briefly forget about my surroundings. But when suddenly interrupted, I have the *ability* to contain myself. Without faulting them, I've had the pleasure of witnessing some who laugh hysterically with torrents of tears coming down their faces and sometimes even falling to the ground.

Without reluctance

Kids have this uncanny *capacity* to laugh without reservation. As soon as they start to recognize and grasp language, laughing is natural for them. Some adults are fortunate enough to possess this childlike experience, while others have to put forth more effort to develop their *capacity* to laugh. From the silliest to the more sublime humor, kids express their laughter in ways adults can't and for things and reasons sometimes unknown to adults.

Laughter is sparked by sensitivities and thoughts. We start laughing from around the age of three to five months old, which shows that our *capacity* for laughing is inborn.

Laughter as a shield

Here are just a few benefits that accompany the *capacity* to laugh:

- It reduces stress hormone levels.
- Increases the flow of blood and oxygen to the cells and organs
- It naturally works several muscle groups, which may be a shield against sickness.
- It can lower your blood pressure.
- Scientists concur that laughter is related to intelligence, enhanced memory, and creativity.
- Simply having the sense of well-being is incentive enough to laugh more.
- We gain a good abs workout.

Relevant links

www.organicfacts.net
www.gaiam.co
www.kidshealth.org
www.nbcnews.com (Robert Provine, PhD)

Capacity to Live Independently

Living self-reliantly can be advantageous for people who opt for a lifestyle of privacy. Another reason for single living might be to try a new routine unencumbered by interruptions that can occur when a roommate is present. You've been bombarded with company! Sometimes it's a great thing. But now, your appreciation for solitude suddenly becomes precious and necessary. Most people do *not* have the *capacity* to be alone for any length of time. Yet solitude is for some a welcome opportunity that affords us these pleasures:

- Breathtaking moments to be refreshed
- Motivation to achieve goals by indulging in our creative selves
- Our minds are more easily stimulated
- There's more time for self-appreciation
- Freedom from the commotion of crowds
- Insight to see the world in a whole new dimension

Youthful pleasures warrant the need for constant companionship; with a more mature perspective and *capacity,* life is vastly different, especially when accomplishing goals is the target. Instead, in an exceptional way, deliberately finding those quiet times is empowering. As a passionate writer, enjoying the benefits of solitude allows time for collecting intimate thoughts. Apart from those moments, opinions shared might not be as fruitful. It is a gratifying achievement to present findings of personal experiences and intensive research to the world, imparting treasures that are sometimes unknown to many.

And while loneliness is usually a path where one is estranged from company, not always because of one's choosing, solitude is a *deliberate desire*, even longing, to be isolated when realizing a dream. But what's alarming is that few have any conception of *what solitude means* and may even be terrified at the thought of being alone.

> In quietness and in confidence shall be thy
> strength. (Isaiah 13:15)

(Relevant link: www.oxfordclinicalpsych.com)

Capacity to Enjoy Life, to Think Freely

Because of mental or emotional restraints, it may be daunting for some to enjoy life and think freely. The *ability* just isn't there. Making a choice to change such a lifestyle can be demanding and stressful. However, when association with the right people is encouraged, the *capacity* to receive support can now be a reality.

It would be inconsistent under these circumstances *not* to acknowledge the truth that God, the supreme Creator, is love and that clear-cut answers are available through him. God is *our sufficiency*. People do find deliverance in areas of their lives that enable them to once again capture or recapture the joys of living. This is when we start to think freely, making decisions that affect us in good ways.

Visualize trusting *only God* to direct our steps and answer our petitions!

The Capacity to Excel

It's been a lifelong query as to why some brilliant entrepreneurs toil and strain to launch their businesses and achieve their goals while others just zoom through the process unscathed. Concentrated education and performance with determination is the secret to success of apparently less skillful individuals.

Requesting help may be taboo

We sometimes tend to feel inadequate in specific areas or when discussing topics where we dare not ask for help or clarification; the *capacity* just isn't there. I've heard it said, "I'd rather *die* than ask for help." In our minds, asking could appear to be a sign of our insufficiency, that we lack knowledge. Managers, teachers, supervisors, and others in authority may deem this lack of asking for help as unwillingness or rejection.

Asking for help as well as giving help can be a means of fostering warm relationships with our peers. However, for employees or students who are reluctant to ask for help on projects at work or school, the giant in the minds of these nonparticipants might be greater than we deem imaginable! A number of reasons for this may be:

- Wanting to be sure the questions asked are sound and reasonable
- Not wanting to taint one's reputation
- Lack of confidence in another person's ability to fulfill the request
- Fear of not wanting to be permanently labeled as incapable

Beneath all of the above is a genuine fear of the unknown.

> For God has not given us the spirit of fear;
> but of power, and of love, and of a sound mind.
> (2 Timothy 1:7 KJV)

So then one can safely conclude that fear comes from *another source*, and it does—*the negative force* of this world, our adversary. *There's nothing our adversary desires more than that we should be ignorant of his devices and presence.*

(Relevant link: www.hbr.org [Harvard Business Review])

Climbing High

Anyone who's ever gone hiking or climbing should be extremely proud of their tenacity. Kudos! The truth is, some of us will not even attempt this adventure, and others will admit they simply do not have the *capacity*, willingness, desire, or ability.

People have been encouraged, persuaded, or sometimes even forced to, but none of these seemed to coax them into participation because of that inhibiting factor dubbed as incapacity. It is inexplicable and cannot be fairly labeled as stubbornness or even trepidation.

Monumental benefits

It could be climbing Mount Everest or a mountain in the state where we live, the thrill and anticipation is about the same. You see, it's not so much the mountain as it is the satisfaction and sense of pride we find in knowing that we have the ability to overcome obstacles and arrive to the top. The physical and mental benefits are monumental and don't cost us much to get away from the hustle and bustle of a typical city life.

Escape sitting at a desk

Researchers at Stanford conducted a study that showed our creativity is heightened by as much as 60 percent as a result of hiking. One study shows that in the US, one in four adults spend at least 70 percent of their time sitting. This habit is strongly linked to having heart disease and the possible risk of cancer.

Breathing fresh air is a plus when hiking and viewing the gorgeous sites that surround us. It's a sure way to lift your mood, especially when you're away from cities that are polluted. Studies also show that this low-impact, fun engagement reduces the risk of hypertension, cholesterol, and type 2 diabetes.

Vacation away from the gym

Hiking falls into quite a different category compared to heavy weight-lifting at a gym, and the experience affords you the time for reflection and leisure. Be as comfortable as you possibly can for this out-of-the-ordinary event by adhering to the rules that accompany having a successful and carefree time. Suitable gear—including comfortable boots and high-quality, durable gym wear—is a must.

(Relevant link: https://goodlifezen.com)

Accepting a Compliment

A genuine compliment can reverse the course of a day for someone. It may *change* one's mood from gloomy to cheerful! Many people tend to have this *natural eye* for discernment and can notice when a compliment is not being graciously accepted. Something inside tells the recipient they may be undeserving or the person showering these compliments may not be honest.

Capacity to give compliments

This is a heartwarming feeling that might also be the same for the recipient. We are not always aware of what an individual might be experiencing at the moment a compliment is being given. But even when knowledgeable, *for some*, it is not in the heart, mind, or *capacity* to even consider putting forth the effort to compliment someone. Here are some conclusions that may satisfy this conduct:

- Having never received a compliment
- Having been severely mistreated
- Those given were not genuine
- Concluding that compliments are futile

Compliments when sincere have the power to change the lives of individuals who might otherwise feel inadequate or miserable. Picture stretching one's *capacity* to emulate this pattern that may make a small positive impact in the life of another!

Transcending Our Capacity

When we've reached the edge of what we consider our *capacity*, there's a foolproof dimension that defies the explanation that *capacity* is unchangeable. It comes from multiple sources over centuries.

Power to dethrone

Having a close relationship with God Almighty is easy and is the answer to transcending our capacities and abilities. We only have to be willing and bold enough to approach him and express our desire to be close to him. Only he has the power to overthrow the weaknesses that afflict us. He loves and cares for us as he said in his Word. It is also stated in the Bible that...

> God is not a man that He should lie.
> (Numbers 23:19 KJV)

We can trust Him because of the following:

- He is the *only* source for truth.
- He created the world, *all things*, and is *still* in charge despite appearances.
- When we embrace his Word and take the necessary actions, the rewards can be jaw-dropping!
- Billions of people over centuries have proved all of the above to be accurate; these are people who have not allowed their eyes to be blinded by fabrication.

- Surprising evidences point to God's astounding and never-ending love for humanity.

As we stand shoulder to shoulder with the reality that God is truly the one that has the power to dethrone our enemy, we'll have the *ability* to stand firm on our convictions and see the desired results.

The Monster We Face

Here's something most of us have had to face at least once in life—
forgiveness. When we have the *capacity* and *ability* to be forgiving,
as *demanding* as it might be, we *escape* agony and further grief. This
affords us the liberty to *celebrate* a new beginning. We're now traveling light.

And another thing...

The longer we "wait," the harder it becomes, the farther away we
are from closure and liberation. We cannot claim true contentment
when this demon is looming in our space. By our holding on to
this emotion, we can most assuredly *tolerate*, but there will always be
the realization that something is lacking—not a pleasant feeling. We
can't afford to do less than embrace having closure.

No worries

Getting our victory is just *one thought* away. Exercising freedom of
will is somewhat like getting out of bed in the morning when we'd
rather be sleeping; it's one step out at a time. Just dream about having
to exercise "*discipline*" (that dreadful word, for most of us), which is
the foundation for everything we do daily!, from brushing our teeth
to taking our dog out for a walk.

But since freedom of will dominates every decision we make,
we have the upper hand to manipulate our heart's desires, and with
God as our refuge and strength, we're not alone in our decision-mak-

ing. One of his promises is that he will never leave us, making the process simpler. There's always a way out because God loves us, and based on his Word, it's more than we can or ever will conceive.

Let's face it, forgiving is the only way to go when we've been wronged in any way. The person we forgive may be the one suffering the most, having severe remorse for bad decisions they may have made. Others that aren't remorseful we just commit them to God who handles things in the most efficient ways.

Maintaining Our Capacity

When we're determined to be *inflexible* in areas where we definitely want to grow, we've confined ourselves to a mental box. Of course, an unperturbed attitude may be just a comfort-zone alternative for many. And we frequently resort to that rather than have our "feathers ruffled," either by being convinced we're unable to make the shift or unwilling to do so.

Fulfillment of a longing

As a teenager, before I rode my first bicycle, I was *fixed* with the notion that this may never happen. But I launched out after seeing friends and family just like me riding bikes; their encouragement motivated me, and I realized how much I was missing. I fulfilled a longing and was bursting with exhilaration, having done something I enjoyed that was new and exciting.

So feeling the breeze on my face while riding was well worth it, especially when I realized I was simultaneously gaining all the benefits of exercise. I stretched beyond my *capacity* and my *ability* followed. In the years that followed, riding became one of my most cherished pastimes.

Captivated by My Peers

We commonly regard this as a disease that infects teenagers, but let's face it, most people effortlessly "follow the crowd" when their reputations might be jeopardized. We tend to be absorbed in these attractions:

- Interests
- Habits
- Traditions
- Religious affiliation
- Political affiliation
- Neighborhood standards
- And other things

It sometimes takes bravery and a sense of individuality to resist doing what might be considered the norm in these instances. No one wants to be deemed "different." This may accurately be defined as being *held captive*, not *merely* a teenage obstacle. Maturity as we know is not reliant on age but on a dynamic acumen to rise above the standard of the clique.

Having the *capacity* to separate from the norm is not always an easy choice. But millions have dared to take the stand for something that's indispensable and have achieved *astounding victories* as a result. *Uniqueness is a force that displays to them who we really are, so we cannot compromise our lifestyle based on the opinions or codes of others.*

What has always puzzled me about some who've claimed to be unique (one of a kind) is that they, maybe unconsciously, emulate others and not in subtle ways. There's nothing wrong with that.

Believe it or not, we do need one another. In our natural *capacity* is that desire to imitate one another to some degree.

Peer pressure can be a positive force when we surround ourselves with people who uphold worthwhile values. Developing friendships with people regardless of their age, religious or economic backgrounds, or ethnicity adds treasured enrichment to our lives.

One of the greatest examples of someone that did not succumb to pressure by his peers was Jesus Christ. Yes, when they may have strayed at times, he had to bring his disciples back to the reality of life on earth, but he didn't follow in their footsteps.

> He was in all points tempted like as we are,
> yet without sin. (Hebrews 4:15 KJV)

(Relevant links: www.scholastic.headsup.com)

Capacity to Trust

On the planet in which we live, we've experienced these sentiments at different times—some or all of them:

- Assuming
- Innocent
- Committed
- Dependent
- *Trusting*
- Guessing
- Gullible
- Confident
- Expecting
- Naive
- Presuming
- Suspicious

Each of these expresses in some way our *trust* or apprehensions to make decisions that affected us in numerous ways.

Enviable trust

Very young children are generally *unassuming* and *innocent*; they trust just about everyone, especially their parents and care providers. Their *capacity* to trust is *enviable*, but they're also *naive* and not normally *suspicious* of their surroundings or of other people. They are totally *dependent* on others and *expect* and deserve only absolute comfort and guidance.

Adults are knowledgeable, but some of us make crucial commitments that engage the reciprocation of another person. We become *suspicious* when these promises fall short of our expectations.

Trustworthy and dependable source

Perhaps you've already guessed that there is a source of trustworthiness that has *no boundaries*. This has been attested by *billions over several centuries*. God—the Creator of heaven, earth, and all things—is the *only reliable source* that we can turn to. Others continue to fail after much trial and error! So why isn't everyone hyped up about this *amazing* truth?

You see, there is *also* an opposing source called the adversary, who is ever present and whose *only purpose* is to *blind the eyes* of many. Just imagine when someone is unresponsive to the Creator of *all things*, then the conclusion is crystal clear—blindness! Who would venture to trust anyone else.

Our vilest opponent

It feels so much safer to *evade* the likelihood of having to acknowledge that we are constantly targeted by *the archenemy of all life*. There's a *hush* whenever the subject is raised, but we don't have to look very far to agree that there's a force much greater than the strongest of us. Throughout the Bible, our foe is spoken of in direct and indirect terms. *This is no secret:*

> The thief cometh not but for to steal, kill
> and destroy. (John 10:10)

His only agenda. This includes our joy and health, a wholesome family life, freedom to be prosperous, or anything else that might bring us happiness—something we all have a hankering for.

build layer upon layer as you experimented. For him, it was immense fun and a complete distraction. He added that it also amplified his *capacity* to see. Traveling afforded him the pleasures to embrace his hobby, and he painted approximately six hundred works of art during his lifetime.

Painting something seemingly insignificant

There is so much to capture from nature's beautiful splendor: landscapes, rivers, waterfalls, flowers and birds—the selection is perpetual. What might seem to be an insignificant object might be exactly what a painter needs for his canvas. Beauty in the eye of the beholder can be discovered anywhere.

Portrait painters strong as ever

With digital camera photography so prominent, portrait painters still hold their heads up high; the genre is distinctly different. This immortal art cleverly restores the old and gives acceptance to the new. Although photography has taken center stage in our society, portrait artists are highly revered as the forerunners in capturing the images of people. Their popularity has not diminished but increased. Their *ability* to charm the minds of their audience continues to be magnetic.

Irreplaceable gift item

There's something inexplicably fascinating about seeing oneself on canvas. For many, this appreciation stems from the awareness of the time, effort, and dedication it takes to produce such a work of art. It is irreplaceable in that there's not another that will be identical, although it might come pretty close. Portraits are treasured for many reasons; it takes a *capacity* of inventiveness to produce an almost perfect portrait. Portraits are heirlooms that are also prized as expensive gift giving.

Relevant links

www.diversityabroad.com
www.huffingtonpost.com (Don Meyer, PhD)
www.express.co.uk

Respecting Capacity

The more we go through life, the more aware we become of our own shortcomings and that of others. Limitations that we observe in others may sometimes stimulate either a yearning to be *supportive or analytical.* When the cry is loud to be tolerant toward another person's *capacity* to perform in an area in which we are expert, we want to respond with compelling actions that effortlessly and willingly step up to their call for empathy and emotional support.

Deliberate actions

Whatever the reason for one's inadequacy, an honest *respect* can be displayed on the part of the person who offers brave and straightforward inspiration. Extraordinary gratification is felt when deliberate actions are taken to *reveal* and improve the talents of others.

Important points that we want to remember:

- We all have shortcomings.
- Not everyone is interested in stretching their *capacity.*
- We want to rise up when the demand is apparent.
- People are generally receptive and zealous about improving their lives.

Authorized health professionals like doctors, psychologists, social workers, occupational therapists, or nurses should be consulted when determining the extent to which someone is able or agreeable to change.

(Relevant link: www.nsbs.org)

Capacity to Be Satisfied

There *seems* to be in most of us an inborn demand for more. Although that's not true of everyone, many of us are insatiable beings who are *content* to justify cravings for material things that might exhibit our status in a society or community.

Even when credit cards have reached their limits, purchases continue! This is a national drawback that we've tolerated for long enough *to not want "out."* "Living within our means" has become a trite expression. We might say why would we want to do that anyway? You see, *bondage* comes wrapped up with a beautiful bow, but sooner or later, we have to unwrap the package!

Perplexing conclusions

This craving for more, like many other traits we acquire, cannot always be explained; it is simply a reality of life. Conversely, there are individuals who, in spite of the lures and enticements of peer pressure, seem to be unbending in their determinations to not fall prey.

This may be *overwhelmingly* easier said than done for many, since *capacity* varies in each individual. So then it's a matter of discretion and a sense of what is essential for our lifestyle.

The worthwhile possibility

A genuine realization of an *intimate relationship with God,* when practiced, subdues passions and allows us the *ability* to embrace *the* peace that bypasses typical *understanding.* When peace is enforced, we are not compelled or goaded by competitors; rather, we're free to make choices based on our own reasonable motivations. Nothing beats having the *capacity* to own our freedom in every aspect of life!

Candy Jar on the Coffee Table

It was guaranteed; that large shiny crystal glass jar was always await-ing my sweet tooth! I could imagine the up-and-down movements of her jaws as she vigorously jumped on the trampoline. She's in her nineties! Her *capacity* to resist sweets like bonbons seems to be unrestricted.

My *adorable* aunt Lillis—a gentle and kind soul—tried on many occasions to abandon her craving. Now many years later, she's chosen to store her candy in the freezer and control her intake to *"one a day."* *It makes me smile to think about it.*

The stretch that empowered her

This was not easy, but the *desire* to become healthier by cutting down her consumption of candy overruled her *urge*. This was a *total stretch*, but she succeeded and sticks with her plan. Apparently, the potential for change was *latent* even though she lacked the *capacity* to drive herself. I respect her difficult decision but can almost feel a *sense of guilt* seeing (amusingly) mind pictures of her possibly digressing.

Capacity to Endure Criticism

We're acclaimed for our courage, strength, and "thick skin," yet there's just one criticism to which we're *unmistakably* vulnerable! It's different for each of us. What a blow we've been dealt! There are several ways in which we can keep our cool. Here are some tidbits:

- We learn new things and grow tremendously from the suggestions of others. It was once noted that "no man is an island."
- Valuable information sometimes comes in the guise of criticism.
- Humility is realizing our inadequacies by acceptance and change in our course.
- It's best not to analyze the tone in which the criticism was delivered.
- *No one* said it was easy!
- When criticism is false, we can choose to ignore it and be silent.
- Instead of taking it personally, respect and welcome it.
- Maintain your good humor and never respond instantly.

I once wrote an article for a client who was critical of my grammar. My initial response was *not a feeling of severe uneasiness* since the opposite is true of most of my clients. The moment I read her criticism, I felt a tinge of resentment and a sensation much like tiny needles painlessly pressing against my skin. "Who's perfect?" I contended with myself. "What was she talking about?" I thanked her for her business, and successfully delivered the project without responding to the criticism.

Acceleration of growth

Sometimes, we take much for granted and ignore the truth that *not everyone is going to like what we do.* So if we're not careful, we can miss out on opportunities to excel, which may come as a result of accepting helpful criticism.

Now, as we'd suspect, stretching our *capacity* to endure criticism is *quite a stretch!* Yet it might well be worth the effort and time required. Essentially, it's a matter of accelerating our growth to arrive at where we aspire to be is what's most essential.

(Relevant link: www.lifehack.org)

Uttered Blunders or Missteps

Diverse perceptions

It should come as no surprise to us that empty gossip has often been the *cradle that embraces the birth of numerous ills*. Yet research has shown that some have *seized the concept* that gossip can be positive in some ways, such as release stress; provide a source for venting your true concerns; and may foster teamwork, to name only three. Their conclusion was that talking behind someone's back shouldn't always be regarded as a bad thing.

One study at Stanford University confirms that when people collaborate during gossip, they can align information gained in their findings about the behavior of employees to clarify issues.

Exposure of the detriments

First, we should ask this question: "Would I say this in the presence of the person being spoken about?" In light of the above opinions, we rely solely on the integrity of God and his Word. Results based on centuries-long experiences of gossip *clearly expose* its detriments, including but not limited to these:

- It causes stress.
- Triggers divisions in home and family relations
- Instigates backbiting and whisperings
- Is inflammatory and damaging

- Is destructive to both parties; no one is growing up intellectually, spiritually, or otherwise

Unexpected gossip

We should *never* be surprised if gossip is entertained in Christian circles. Why? *Christians are people too.* This is a daily walk with God, and people are *not* usually changed overnight, but the alternative cannot be compared to living this Christian life. We become stronger daily as we study God's Word and appropriate it to our lives.

The concept of gossip is appalling, head-scratching, and has been misunderstood for centuries. Jesus Christ had *to correct or reprove* such people on several occasions to address the many morally weak areas in their lives. There's *nothing new* under the sun in our day and time. We, nevertheless, have an adversary whose business it is to blind the eyes of the uninformed.

An *incredible* characteristic of God is that he is *generously merciful* to Christians and non-Christians alike! It is *critically frustrating* to comprehend all of this without a knowledge of what Jesus Christ did when he gave his life for all. Those who have accepted him as Lord and Savior have eternal life. However, we have this promise from God that at the return of Jesus Christ, we'll all be changed. That's something to look forward to!

Growth requires care and time

The thing is that after receiving Jesus Christ as Lord and Savior with the conviction that God raised him from the dead, *our capacities and personalities don't automatically change overnight. The spirit of God that is in us is perfect*, but we have to work at daily *renewing our minds* by appropriating his Word to our lives.

This is a lifelong process, and people tend to condemn themselves or be disappointed about their behavior since they expect instant change, which is not realistic. Some grow up faster than others in appropriating the knowledge of God to their lives. Allow him to be the judge of us all.

The breakdown in a solid relationship with God can be the source of gossip; resentments may escalate for any reason, and rumors can get started. True disciples of the Lord Jesus Christ wouldn't engage. The *capacity* to refrain can be challenging for most of us, but the *ability* doesn't change.

We can trust God to be with us, closer than our breath, to follow through on the things he asks of us. Is it rational to believe that He would *not* ask us to do something that's impossible?

> The words of a talebearer are as wounds, and they go down into the innermost parts of the belly. (Proverbs 18:8 KJV)

Relevant links

www.psychologytoday.com
www.bigthink.com
www.careerstonegroup.com
www.thehopeline.com

Unparalleled Loyalty

Contingent upon where our loyalty lies is the crux of how we're assessed by the world. A *capacity* for loyalty may be latent in all of us, but how we exercise it reveals our true personality and what we value as the lifeblood of our existence. For instance, some people are first loyal to their spouse, family, friends, employer, and to God—not necessarily always in that order.

Social media loyalty—a bold comparison

Another example is our immense loyalty to the media. These tools *undoubtedly* enhance the quality of our lifestyle by making it easier, and the extent of our loyalties differ from person to person. It would be remiss to ignore the *striking contrast* between the reliability of social media and the trustworthiness of an eternal God.

At times our *iPhone* is affixed to our hip. It's what keeps us in touch with the world around us, and we wouldn't dream of surviving without it (even if we could). We have the *ability* to always call upon God when other *connections* fail.

- *Facebook* may be one of our best friends; almost everyone in the world has an account. We are connected with the people we care about in ways we would not otherwise.

God is our BFF (best friend forever)

And if you have the *capacity* to endure having others see what you had for breakfast or how often you changed your baby's diaper on any given day, it's all right. Freedom of will is an amazing thing!

- *Twitter* keeps us informed by quickly connecting us around the globe. A slight drawback is the 140-character limitation, especially if we always have more to say.

With God, we're never limited to number of words used; we can endlessly call upon him in time of need or *just to have a hearty conversation*. Even though he is not on Twitter, we can still follow Him. There's always a guaranteed direct connection to our heavenly Father.

- When we're connected to *WI-FI* or *Bluetooth high-speed* Internet transmissions and other devices, we relish the ease and flexibility of using our computers and other devices.
- We're passionate about how we look, and *Instagram* accommodates us with the pleasure of selfies, and we indulge in ways never dreamed possible. It also serves to promote our businesses, see what people like, and expand our social platform. God is everywhere, readily available *in a flash* to meet our needs.

Gratification in Service

The world seriously needs our life and *abilities*, and we're responsible for what God has entrusted to us. The depth of our love for him and what he's done for us stimulates us to serve others. The selfish side of us *sometimes pleads* to be the ones being served. For example, an annual vacation is the time to escape the humdrum, run-of-the-mill existence, to forget about doing what some might call menial tasks, like vacuuming, cooking meals, or taking care of young children. "This is it!" we say—our *capacity* to delay is now strained!

Relaxing with the remote and unfamiliar

It's time to explore *the unknow*n, to make new discoveries in this exciting adventure we call vacation. We anticipate being served our food, drinks, and anything else that reminds us that we're now in an entirely remote kingdom, far from what we're accustomed to.

We feel entitled! And we should. We've toiled, sweated, and have been awaiting this for the past year or longer. We now look forward to *being served* in every aspect possible.

Reversing the role

Constrained by financial obligations, we may be the providers of such services yet lack the *capacity* for that position—it's not what we want to do. Serving others can be challenging, especially when the recipients are unappreciative or take service for granted. Our service to God requires commitment and a desire to follow in the footsteps of Jesus Christ. Billions of people over centuries have, by freedom of will, turned their lives to God. The cycle continues with a desire to continue in his ways.

For many, there is this inexplicable yearning to do his will and serve him. As recipients of his numerous blessings, we can't help but reciprocate by listening to the needs of others and teaching them how to turn from darkness to light.

> With good will doing service, as to the Lord,
> and not men. (Ephesians 6:7 KJV)

Slow to Anger

We don't want our mental circuits to be jammed. We guard our minds by focusing the way football players do. In order to win the game and become the champions, they must have the *capacity* and *ability* to strategize. With binding determination, they hasten to own the ball and follow through to a victorious end.

Relentless hard work and willpower lead them to the conquest they deserve. One might think the comparison is simplistic, but just like these players, it takes *one thought at a time*. Anything we want to successfully accomplish requires doggedness, and this method of controlling anger shouldn't be the exception.

Realistic implications to ponder

Professional clinical intervention is necessary for individuals who might lack the *capacity* for change, or they may not be willing to do so. We cannot assume that even under horrific conditions people might want to change. It would be a dismal task trying to estimate the many reasons why we become angry, but a few are worth thinking about:

- We feel disrespected, insulted, or tricked.
- We've been taken advantage of.
- We're retaliating for lack of empathy or helpfulness in a situation.
- Road rage is a common anger.
- Anything that might deter your progress when in haste

The angry person usually doesn't have the time or *capacity* to reason that these accusations may not have been maliciously done. Fresh insight into this subject can effect radical change and have a vital impact in the lives of generations to come. It just takes one member in a family or an individual with gumption to prove that *being in control of one's mind* is the will of God. Continuous encouraging universal results verify that this is realistic.

Proverbs 16:32 makes a bold and powerful biblical statement. Wow!

> He that is slow to anger is better than the
> mighty; and he that rules his spirit than he that
> takes a city.

This implies that, unless clinical intervention is compulsory, we have the *ability* to comply with the suggestion presented here. The outcome for doing what is suggested by God is *always rewarding* to us and the lives of those we touch.

(Relevant link: www.mentalhealth.net)

The Capacity to Believe

Exclusion of this topic would be gross negligence on my part, as it is at the core of my being. God has placed within each of us this *capacity* to *believe* in him; otherwise, he'd be a respecter of persons. We wouldn't all have access to his gift of salvation to all of mankind if anyone lacked this *capacity*. But because of this, we have the *honor* of becoming his children—Christians (Christ in us).

The only way we achieve this is by *believing* that Jesus Christ lived on earth to be our example, was crucified, died, *but God raised him from the dead*. We then *willingly* invite him into our lives and with our mouth confess him as Lord. In that instant, we're now a Christian. It's that easy.

He's not concerned about whether we're on our knees, up at an altar, or at home in a closet. The place or time is irrelevant to him. He loves us so much and only wants us to live life to the fullest, free from the worries and cares of this world. When we take this most important step, we're now snatched from the paws of the enemy and are starting a new life.

Believing *is a law* that works for Christians and non-Christians alike. Everything we want to successfully accomplish hinges on our *believing*. We've seen non-Christians accomplish great things as well. So *why bother to change and* believe in God? Because of the *treasures that are* available to us *now* as Christians and in the end, *everlasting life!* He's a God of *love and mercy*.

> He causes his sun to rise on the just and the unjust, and sends rain on the righteous and the unrighteous. (Matthew 5:35 KJV)

His mercy is everlasting and his truth
endures to all generations. (Psalm 100:5 KJV)

So why not *focus our believing on God*, who created all things and has all the answers? It's an *amazing* privilege we have to completely entrust our lives to him and follow his Word.

When we set out to accomplish our goals and ambitions, we have a resource that's unlimited. We can scale to infinite heights far beyond what our minds can imagine, and we are developing the character of a champion. His Word says that his nature is *not to lie*; he has no reason to—*he's God!* So we can totally trust his Word.

And all things whatsoever ye shall ask in
prayer, believing, ye shall receive. (Matthew
21:21 KJV)

Capacity to Keep a Secret

One of the most revered and honorable thing in this world is having the *capacity* to be entrusted with the deepest secrets of people that either respect or love us. Often, out of desperation, people who deserve respect and trust divulge their most intimate thoughts and sometimes to the least worthy. Then, unfortunately, that trust is broken and bitterness ensues.

The thing is, most people don't normally plan to reveal what they're asked not to, but there seems to be *dormant* within us this curiosity just waiting to surface, to see the reactions of those we tell. As human beings, we do err.

A conflict of interest

Even trusted employees of large establishments are sometimes exempted from knowing secrets that might pose a conflict of interest. For example, a centuries-old recipe of a restaurant that is a family's inheritance might be the target. Though it may take a strong effort to *withhold* private information, it is not necessarily impossible to do so. In some cases, it may be quite easy to keep a secret for the first time, but the drive to make this a habit is nonexistent.

The uneasiness of betrayal

When asked to unveil confidential matters, some express a feeling of guilt and would rather tell a lie than bear the uneasiness of betrayal. There's an old saying that goes like this: "Ask me no questions, and

I'll tell you no lies." Then there's the thrill that some may experience in the knowledge of having information that no one else knows about. When this is entrusted to the wrong person, it is used as a tool for extortion, bribery, or other corruption, like blackmail.

Just enjoy the movie

By giving away the plot of a movie *before it's been seen*, avid moviegoers put a damper on the anticipation and enjoyment of the event. This is such a temptation for many and could be derived from the desire to always have a heads-up above others. I say this very politely: we just want to enjoy the movie! Having a well-guarded "lockbox" is a choice that we can make. Whether the secret is a good or bad one, having the guts to refrain from *what appears to be the norm* is an admirable trait.

> Trust in the Lord with all thine heart;
> and lean not unto thine own understanding.
> (Proverbs 3:5 KJV)

The truth is there's *no one else* that we can completely trust. *God is our best friend.* Most of us have been deceived or disappointed *at least once* in our lives; others, even more. Our security is *guaranteed* in God. *Finally,* there's someone we can trust with our secrets and every facet of our lives!

(Relevant link: www.fastcompany.com)

Warranted Comparison
The Capacity to Ignore

It would be *defiant* to ignore the truth that everyone is unique and possesses qualities, gifts, and talents that differ from one person to the other. Having the *capacity* to be comfortable in one's skin is satisfying and leads to a life of contentment. Unwarranted comparison carries with it needless burdens:

- Having to extend lines of credit
- Constantly monitoring others
- Working overtime or working several jobs
- Living beyond one's means

For some people, the essence of their existence thrives on comparing themselves with others: who owns the better car, home; who is more financially established; and a slew of other issues.

The ladies we can't forget

When we compare ourselves to others, we run the risk of becoming resentful. Refraining from this behavior is one of the *toughest* things. As kids, our parents may have shown preference for one sibling over another. At school, our work is judged alongside the competence of our classmates. All our lives, *we compare* and are being compared. This is just a fact of life that cannot be ignored. While *necessary* information may be gained from comparison, more often than not, it incites unhappiness and unanswered questions.

High school presents a bundle of anticipations; one was meeting some of my schoolmates for the first time. These women appeared to have everything. As I got to know them, I discovered that not only were they exceptionally beautiful inside and out, *by any standard*, and they were smart. But they had such great personalities and seemed to be naively unaware of their looks—that certainly helped! Youthfulness can flood us with such giddiness that at times we may forget who we are.

The staring contest

I vividly recall the *staring contest*—two of these women decided they'd go for it and started a lunch-free session, which lasted the full hour. The rest of us had eaten and were back in our seats while these were still in competition. They had the *capacity* to engage in this silly joke, which might be painstaking for most of us. Our professor eventually came along and sternly interrupted the fun. While some people stare just out of curiosity, with *no hidden agenda*, my friends took it to the next level; they engaged for the entire lunch period.

Having the Capacity for Thankfulness

It is helpful to concentrate on and *value* the good things we have. This obviously can't apply to everyone, but for a majority of us, this is true:

- We're alive and healthy.
- We have family and friends who care about us.
- We have food on our tables.
- We have a job.
- We live in a good, comfortable home.

There's a vast population that lacks the *ability* to be thankful because of destitution in areas of health and finances. They may have the *capacity* and desire but lack the resources, the *ability*.

The underlying force behind unwarranted comparison could be fear. We cringe at the thought of possibly being the runner-up and *worry* that we may sacrifice our social standing. For example, if we play professional sports, we are repetitively bombarded by comparisons of how we play in contrast to other players. This can weigh quite heavily on the emotions and may upset performance if not *wisely* handled.

Why does the grass *always seem* greener on the other side? Another interesting thing to consider when you compare your lives to others is that while you may be displeased with your existence or circumstance, there's someone who is *convinced* that you're living a dream.

> For we dare not make ourselves of the number, or compare ourselves with some that commend themselves; but they measuring themselves by themselves, and comparing themselves among themselves, are not wise. (2 Corinthians 10:12)

Speaking to the Public

Our aim should be to familiarize ourselves with the demographics of our audience. This is one of the keys to giving a stress-free presentation: by being knowledgeable of their likes, dislikes, ethnicities, education, culture, average age, and income.

You've collected all data necessary for your speech and with months of preparation you're motivated. It's the day you've anticipated; you're bursting with energy and are versed on the answers that people are yearning to hear. You like doing PowerPoint presentations, and the screen is set up and ready to go.

This is not your first time as a presenter; you have the *capacity and ability* to engage your audience. Yet those butterflies still flutter around in your stomach. It happens to the experienced as well as the novice and in some cases can be paralyzing. The best thing you can do is just be yourself. Remember, our audience is people who have come to hear and learn from us. They have questions to the answers we've painstakingly researched, thought through, and it's now just a matter of minutes before we're on stage in full view. I find these objectives helpful to keep in mind:

- We're meeting a need for valued information.
- Our audience is responsive; what is the message we want them to take away?
- We're prepared with confidence, motivation, honesty, and a touch of humor, proven ways to engage our eager audience!
- Our purpose and focus is crystal clear.
- We might make a blunder or two—they don't really care.
- There's nothing like being true to ourselves and being ourselves—no one else has our fingerprints!

Make genuine eye contact with your audience. Slow down and pause frequently; *we don't want to rush through our presentation*; it might be an indication that we're more nervous than we might actually be. The projection and tone of our voice and arm or hand movements should vary. This is another way to retain the attention of our audience and adds to ease in presentation.

When we stay committed to the reasonable allotted time expected to speak, the chances of being long-winded might be slim. Embrace feedback! We gain experience by learning ways in which we can improve our ideas as well as our presentation of those ideas.

> Let your speech be always with grace, seasoned with salt, that ye may know how ye ought to answer every man [human being implied]. (Colossians 4:6 KJV)

(Relevant link: www.inc.com)

Capacity to Embrace Older Age

We're going to all get there sooner or later, so having the *capacity* to be content with that knowledge should put a smile on our faces. But not so fast for some! Many women don't even look their age; they seem to have an advantage over those that do. So we consider some alternatives—there aren't very many. Let's surrender to the idea and move ahead with cosmetics (my sister Germaine can show you how). Some resort to plastic surgery. Freedom of will is a powerful tool; we choose how to use it in wisdom and with deliberation of what the outcome might be. We should always count the cost, not only monetarily but emotionally.

Common root of our anxieties

Fear is frequently the root of our inhibitions and anxieties. We might want to think about this biblical verse.

> The fear of man bringeth a snare but whoso putteth his trust in the Lord shall be safe. (Proverbs 29:25 KJV)

There really isn't any other complete answer to fear apart from having the knowledge of God. There's safety within *that* trust. We have the *capacity* to seek solutions, and the answers are accessible to us as we align ourselves with him and ask for guidance. This has worked for thousands of years and generations and remains the same today.

How much can we turn back the clock? Pretty soon, we'll get back to becoming and looking older. There's a time coming *according to God's timetable* when we won't have to think about our physical appearance since it states in the Bible in Thessalonians that we *shall* be changed to perfection, something we've always wanted. In the meantime, I believe we should do whatever builds our self-esteem and promotes our happiness. We can't deny that this is what we all desire!

A new adventure

The many overlooked treasures of life are now becoming magnified and real as we grow older. We want and have the *capacity* to explore and get more acquainted with what we've possibly been missing. We are now planning trips to foreign places, meeting new people, and looking forward to being a grandparent, among numerous other things. I think that this is a brand-new adventure for many. We're simply in a new phase, which can be exciting while we anticipate taking positive actions for the next chapter of our lives.

Enhancement to our emotions

We tend to kick the negatives that plagued us when we were younger. Renewed energy and vision is now the standard we choose. However, not every elderly person can boast of having these lighthearted feelings. An intimate relationship with God the Creator and his son, Jesus Christ can change the trajectory for anyone who desires to accept this winning lifestyle. We can welcome aging with ease and assurance that this natural process brings with it many blessings and rewards. God still loves us even when we're older, and he's no respecter of persons; this is for everyone!

Taking glances back

What a good time to reflect on so very much, realizing ways in which we can make improvements that will further enrich our lives. We aspire to get the things done that we'd left on the "back burner." For women, it might still be that blue cardigan that you'd promised to crochet for your dear uncle or aunt. Dad might still have that unfinished wooden rocking horse in the work shed, but he's older, and he now just plays on the computer instead, oblivious of his intended gift, but you'll finish it for his younger sibling. Nothing here is critical, but you can now eliminate from your mind the reasons why you didn't have the time to complete working on these hobbies.

New scientific technology

One great consolation is that when we *notice younger people*, we should acknowledge the fact that they are people who are also aging. No one on this present earth is immortal. The clock is ticking, and their time too is fast approaching. Their experiences will sure to be about the same as yours. We cannot reverse the clock, but with new scientific technology, many people are opting for ways to stay younger (see the chapter on "Warranted Comparison").

There should be no sense of self-condemnation for trying to improve our looks. There'll always be opposition in life; we have to be sure that our intentions and motives are in the right place and that we're in harmony with God. He is a loving heavenly father who cares about the things we care about.

The key is to stay as fit and robust as possible. So you would want to connect regularly with your health care provider to make sure you're in optimum shape. You want to enjoy life as much as possible, and caring for yourself is one way of getting you there. It's not imaginable to expect to be a blessing to others when we're casual with our health. We're all aiming to get the most from the pleasure of longevity.

The righteous shall flourish like the palm tree: he shall grow like a cedar in Lebanon. (Psalm 92:12 KJV)

Who satisfieth that mouth with good things; so that thy youth is renewed as the eagles. (Psalm 103:5 KJV)

(Relevant link: www.slowaging.org)

Road Rage Incapacity

We're going there! It isn't sound judgment to allow someone else to decide the kind of day we're going to have. It really is totally up to us. Let's face it, while driving our cars on the roads and highways, how many of the people we encounter do we actually know? Yet we sometimes tend to use expletives and *hand or finger* gestures to express our frustration about their driving skills—horn-honking or tailgating (*my pet peeve*). The more modest among us are not as brave or agitated. But somehow, we too sometimes entertain thoughts that are inconsistent with the knowledge of the circumstances people driving on the roads might be facing.

So for the most part, but not generalizing, our *capacity* for coping with road rage is insufficient. *We always want to be the example for the generations to follow. Children notice our behavior and regard it as acceptable.* These impressionable people deserve our attention and mindfulness. Let's consider certain dynamics:

- How can we tell that the person speeding behind the wheel is not a soon-to-be father rushing his pregnant wife to the nearest hospital to deliver their twin babies?
- A student driver may be on the road, not usually a threat; most of us have been novices at one time.
- Someone is in severe pain while trying to get to work on time.
- Running the red light *may* be a sign that there is an emergency.
- The brakes on someone's car might have suddenly gone out, causing the car to accelerate beyond what's normal.

- Someone's brake lights may not be working; they're unaware.
- Construction delays are one of the major causes for road rage.

There's no excuse for someone whizzing in and out of traffic lanes, driving under the influence of liquor or other substances, texting while driving, speeding for the fun of it or for criminal purposes, and other traffic offences.

The milk truck incident

My husband, Phillip, told me about a day many years ago before we met. He was driving at sixty-five miles per hour, crossing a bridge on the freeway when the traffic suddenly merged to one lane and slowed down. The brakes of his car went out, which forced him to speed up. Ahead of him was *the milk truck* with an iron bumper.

Because of the concrete road barriers, he had no choice to go either right or left. The driver behind could be belligerent or patient and supportive. He chose to be supportive. I think this was worth noting since not many of us like to wait even a minute for the red light to change, but that is not considered road rage!

Road rage may reveal a form of narcissism, a need to be in control of the road, an inflated ego, or a desire to feel and act superior to drivers whose cars may not be as pricey. Of course, the number of reasons can be overwhelming.

The results of acting out one's road rage might be due to any of the following:

- Having one's license suspended
- Being cited by police
- Arrested for careless driving
- Causing harm to ourselves and others

When family and others close to us are riding in our car, we have accountability for their comfort and safety. So it's *not worth the struggle* and time involved to make snap decisions that endanger lives. Although we're not perfect, we have the advantage of being *able* at any moment to call upon God, who is closer to us than our breath. He has all the answers and is with us at all times.

> Be strong and of a good courage, fear not,
> nor be afraid of them: for the Lord thy God, he
> it is that doth go with thee; he will not fail thee,
> nor forsake thee. (Deuteronomy 31:6)

Relevant links

www.imtbc.com
www.psychologytoday.com

Manage Sibling Rivalry

For some parents, raising children is a daunting obligation; their *capacity* is not equal to the task before them. So once we add sibling rivalry to the list of things that have to be dealt with, the process becomes far more demanding. To ease the burden and free ourselves from some of the pitfalls that come along, it's advisable to keep these key points in mind:

- Every child wants to believe that he/she is the most appreciated and loved of the family.
- There's uniqueness in each child.
- Partiality should never be shown, but this is tempting when one child displays so much more appealing qualities than another.
- Comparison of appearances, school grades, or talents might cause family rifts.
- Plan family events carefully, especially birthdays and holidays so that one does not stand out as over-the-top by comparison. Lay out rules together and discuss them with your kids. Give them opportunities to have input and feel valued.
- Discussing one child with another instigates conflicts; it is best to avoid this.
- Each child deserves one-on-one time with parents.
- Another thing to keep in mind is that when children are sick and in need of our special care, this could be explained to the others at our discretion if they need to know.

- In mixed families where there's adoption, a child should never be referred to as "stepchild." We don't want our children to endure FOMO (fear of missing out).

Family meetings shouldn't be an intimidating time but should be looked forward to. Set the priorities for discussion and clarify issues to be discussed; have them come up with the best solutions and find ways to make them think. Talk about the fun, exciting, or amusing events of the past few days or any concerns about things that didn't work out as planned. Have them think of ways in which they can improve the previous week.

Relevant links

www.huffingtonpost.com
www.centerforparentingeducation.org
www.drgailgross.com

Capacity to Try Something New

Visit the moon? That's quite an ambitious exploit, and many people are dreaming about it. Some of us just don't have the *capacity* to *stretch* that far for anything that may be risky. It takes courage and determination to attempt a feat. Some of our peers may think we're just eccentric or weird, while others may heartily engage and support our vision. It's best to shun the ones who try to deprive you of your expectations leading up to the big day.

The following ways in which we advance to new levels can be stimulating:

- Simply let go of any inhibitions and pursue our aspirations. When our mind is made up, then we can discover how far we can go. But we'll never know until we take that *first step, the one that's the trickiest. Stretching* our *capacity* to a comfortable level might be a valuable exercise.
- It becomes pretty boring not to explore new ideas and ambitions. Doing new things affords us the opportunity to see vistas that are beyond our imagination.
- We can learn to relinquish the habits of family traditions that hold us back from chasing our ideals. You may just be the first to attempt something that contradicts their ingrained ways of reasoning, and they may discourage you.

If we're satisfied with where we are, we'll be the same place we've always been. For some, that's okay, but for others who tend to feel stifled with the daily routines life offers, they are carefree and unstoppable.

- So be the one who is more than likely to try something novel. Incidentally, people like us are inclined to be continually busy; our calendars are replete with events for every day of the week, and we're *fun to be around*. It is said that "a rolling stone gathers no moss." Time shouldn't be wasted, so activity is the hub of our existence.
- Taking a leap of *believing* is something we singly decide. In the beginning, it may seem like a *lonely road*, but with persistence, we'll realize our aspirations.
- The liberty that spontaneity often affords can catapult us to the next level when we embrace opportunities that are presented. Sometimes they just show up unannounced! We just have to always be ready. These don't happen frequently. Getting a good grasp of what they are and not letting go ignites the flame that keeps us moving forward, *forgetting those things which are behind us*.
- "There's only one way to avoid criticism: Do nothing, say nothing, be nothing" (Aristotle).
- Life may be comfortable; there's no one to compete against, nothing to argue about, nothing *much* to do. There are minimal challenges to face, and life is a breeze when we are not motivated to *try new things*. But what is our contribution to God, others, and ourselves?
- Believe God for the impossible!

(Relevant link: www.inc.com)

Capacity to Work

In my search and research, I found the definition that somewhat satisfies my understanding of these two words: *capacity* versus *ability:*

> Work capacity is the ability to perform real physical work, and work ability is a result of interaction of worker to his or her work; that is: how good a worker is at present, in the near future, and how able is he or she to do his or her work with respect to work demands and health and mental resources.[1]

Unmatched job offers

It would be unrealistic to believe that *all* people work at their full *capacity.* Most of us have done jobs that we weren't passionate about, but for financial reasons, we rode along, accepting the humdrum on a daily basis. Many find jobs that do not match their degrees, abilities, or desires, so they're not driven even when a company offers decent incentives.

While in college, many of us choose courses that may not necessarily relate to our passions, but we make new discoveries along the way. Sometimes it may take several years before we finally realize what our dream job truly looks like. It might have been out of fear that we grabbed the first job we were offered and stuck with it for

---

[1] This was a study done among tea plantation workers in South India (*Indian Journal of Occupational and Environmental Medicine*).

Capacity for Bootlicking

I sometimes amaze myself when I address an issue like *bootlicking!* I could have chosen other *similar* words, but I just love boots; they're quite cool. But seriously, my determination for *hitting on this topic* is the fact that it is a *centuries-old practice* started since the beginning of human existence, and one that has *always either* disgusted or *amused* me as I looked on. It releases my adrenaline, so I thought I'd get right to it. My lifelong *capacity* for tolerance in this *arena* is immensely low!

The best alternative

Writing about this subject was not just an overnight decision. I believe it stems from when we were young kids; my parents advocated never "begging" for things. Since then, this concept has caused me to ponder. We were taught how to *pray and believe God* for anything we wanted, and I believe we turned out pretty good.

> Ask, and ye shall receive, that your joy may be full. (John 16:24 KJV)

There's quite a difference between *asking* and *begging*. Our *joy will be full* when the answers to our prayers are realized. There's *nothing more fulfilling* in life than to accomplish our dreams and see the desires of our hearts come to pass—all without a need to beg.

We can be well positioned

Imagine how we can be passionately convinced that we're where God wants us to be and that he's *smart enough* to position us wherever we need to be—anywhere and at any time! When we rely on others instead of the one true God, then there's collapse, and we're sometimes disappointed. We trust in people to some extent but *absolutely trust in God at all times.* And we love all people unconditionally, not walking around suspiciously since that would be futile. *We need one another,* "no man is an island." We just need to walk circumspectly, not deceived.

Gender impact in the workplace

The reason for bringing up the *absolute trust in God* idea is my recollection of having worked for a few of the largest corporations and influential people in the United States. Genders intertwine in the workplace; temptations will always be a part of life. There's no escaping them, but how we *choose* is what matters most.

When we encounter a situation that's unsettling, we can't afford to *bootlick* or succumb to fear but rather *act*: pray, believe, and stand our ground, *trusting God* to *defend* what is true, honest, *just, pure, lovely,* and of good report based *only* on his Word (Philippians 4:8). As we know, none of us is perfect, so we rely on him to direct our steps every *moment* of the day. This takes being in close communication with God, not just for the start or end of but throughout the day!

Bold behaviors of bootlickers

Here are some ways people may indulge in this behavior by targeting someone in a superior position:

- They flatter the target for *no* valid reason.
- They're *unwilling* to be honest.

- They *imitate their target*, which is great *when profitable and done for self-improvement*, but the line should be drawn when gestures, habits, and quirks are also imitated.
- They exhibit *low self-esteem* by bowing to every request even when they don't agree.
- Bootlickers *pretend* to like the ideas and things their target likes.

They might be afraid of losing their job or not hitting the jackpot in the *kingdom of rivalry*. What a burdensome life to live! The *best alternative* promises freedom from intimidation, which is what this is all about. "Fear is sand in the machinery of life." What's unfortunate is that they don't believe they have the backbone or *capacity* to alter their conduct, so they persist, causing embarrassment to themselves and furthermore, *in some cases,* inflating the egos of their targets.

Simplify Our Lives

Do we have the *capacity* to simplify our own lives? We often do an admirable job, showing others ways to make their lives *a breeze*. For example, we give out information on how to downsize their dwellings; carpool to work with someone instead of driving; advise them to do their shopping online instead of rushing off to the mall; and in making other major, positive decisions.

If our focus on our own streamlining was the same as we expend to others, we'd finish so much more by not taking ourselves for granted. We often believe we'll get it all done on time. For some reason, when it comes to simplifying our own lives, we're stunned by the path we often take. We frequently overestimate our *capacity* and are reluctant to attack tasks that have been on the "back burner."

Finishing one chore at a time

We can't do it all, so let's maintain a safe pace. Otherwise, we could be stumbling around trying to meet deadlines that don't concern us and becoming disappointed when we're unable to do so. It starts by trying not to keep up with everyone else. Most people can't *effectively* multitask; the most important of all chores sometimes gets missed. It's admirable when multitaskers finish each task with one-hundred-percent satisfaction.

Finishing *one job at a time* and seeing it to completion is achievable and leaves less room for slipups. Although it *might* take a little more time, how gratifying it is when a job is unquestionably well done.

Saying no without compunction

Learning to politely say "no" is a challenge for many of us. We shoulder responsibilities that could just as easily be assigned to someone else. Other reasons for not having the *capacity* to say "no" may be as follows:

- We might lose the companionship of a friend.
- Our kids might not approve of our decisions; we cherish their love and adoration.
- We don't want to turn down social invitations; other invited guests might think *we weren't invited.*
- We just feel bad about saying "no."

We really don't have to give a lengthy explanation as to why we are unable to accept a task or attend a function, especially if it's not profitable for us or our family. We may want to spend that time with the people closest to us as we may have been apart for a while.

You don't have to say that you're "busy" (a word that is overused). You're "occupied" *that day or at that time* (just not in the same way some might be).

Saying yes when help is offered is another way to unwind and gracefully accept. It could mean the answer to having a nice evening out with a spouse or friend, as opposed to completing a stressful project. We might notice upon returning home that the assignment might seem lighter! Taking healthy breaks add to the enjoyment of a day, and it *simplifies* our lives.

Each life is precious to God, so as we make choices that are unselfish and worthwhile, he often places the right people in our paths, mainly those in dire need of him and his Word. All we have to do is weigh our priorities, giving him first place. The outcome of living this way is always fulfilling to us and the lives we touch.

The major crutches that bind us

Another way to *simplify our life* is by *not* purchasing things that we can't easily afford. This is where that dreadful word "discipline" takes us to a higher level. As we take that *first* leap with determination, we find that the *second* is a tad easier. We may now become enlightened to the reality that "this is how it really works." If we keep up the pace, we'll be well on our way to a surprising victory!

Major *crutches may complicate* our lives as we heedlessly embrace them. We *must* plug in our chargers; endlessly check our e-mails (we could *unsubscribe* to many of these) and tweets, for "fear of missing out" (FOMO); and of course, not disappoint our Facebook friends who eagerly and may repetitively check our posts.

The convenience of having all these options available to us is unmatched, yet it's possible to uphold a balance between what our true *needs* are as compared to our *wants*. Both are vitally important, and we *may be able to* exercise the *capacity to keep both in check*.

Another *good* way we can simplify our lives is by being persistent about maintaining our health spiritually, mentally, and physically. Let's stay connected to our maker, God, by reading, studying, and *living* his Word. With the same vigor, we can also drastically lower our medical bills as we eat healthily and exercise often.

An invaluable plan

Connecting with God first daily is an *invaluable plan* to ensure that our lives are *in balance*. We owe it to ourselves so we can be armed for what can at times be a day of struggle. To the naked eye, it may feel like we're wrestling with people, but the following verse gives *some* insight as to the real competition:

> For we wrestle not against flesh and blood,
> but against principalities, against powers, against
> the rulers of the darkness of this world, against

spiritual wickedness in high places. (Ephesians 6:12)

When we take care of our minds by entertaining thoughts that are in harmony with what God thinks about us, we can enjoy freedom from confusion, doubts, and fears. Our entire being, which includes our mind, is special to God and worthy of our attention.

He cares that we stay healthy and productive so that we can give our best to ourselves and others. When we work together with him as our coach, we can do exploits and reap the benefits of our giving.

> Finally, brethren, whatsoever things are true, whatsoever things are honest, whatsoever things are just, whatsoever things are pure, whatsoever things are lovely, whatsoever things are of good report; if there be any virtue, and if there be any praise, think on these things. (Philippians 4:8 KJV)

Costly and disheartening result

How *delightful* that most of us have the *capacity* to *appropriate our financial resources in better ways*! It can be costly and disheartening trying to recuperate from sicknesses, diseases, and financial losses as a result of unwise spending.

> Beloved I wish above all things that thou mayest prosper and be in health even as thy soul prospers. (3 John: 2 KJV)

Relevant links

www.huffingtonpost.com (simplify your life)
www.theblissfulmind.com (simplify your life)

Humane Capacity: Caring for Our Pets

The level of emotional heaviness and strain can be devastating when caring for a sick pet. It is closely comparable to the care of a child since many pets are respected as family members. It is also known that for many, having a pet may not only be therapeutic in providing companionship, but statistics prove that our national population embraces the ownership of pets.

Comfortable care considerations

Readiness and selection of a pet is as much an enormous undertaking as the adoption of a child and in some cases *may be even more so* based on the condition of the pet. Well-known precautions are worth repeating to serve as reminders. We love our pet but lack the *capacity* to comfortably care for them *in every aspect*. When this is the case, serious consideration should be given to alternatives.

Now just imagine for a moment having to ensure that our pet is free from discomfort, pain, injury, and diseases! Plus…

- Having thorough and regular vet checkups, including vaccination
- Monitoring health on a daily basis
- Maintaining a clean, sheltered environment
- Keeping our pets hydrated by refilling water bowl regularly
- Providing highly nutritious food
- Making sure exercise is a normal part of the day
- Demanding that they follow simple commands

- Dental care and good grooming
- Neutering if we're not interested in pet breeding

Habitual social interactions with our pet will result in a friendly and fun relationship.

When pets are caged, the surface on which they're placed should be at least three inches in soft thickness. Comfortable temperatures should be about sixty to eighty degrees Fahrenheit. An adequately large litter box is preferred for ease in mobility, also a designated area for eating and sleeping away from excretion—but instead, a clean dry environment. One may have the *potential and ability* to perform such tasks but may not be convinced they have the *capacity*.

Relevant links

www.petpoint.com
www.cbsnews.com
September 19, 2017 Alan Mozes

Two More Points of Interest

I've included the following two topics that complement the meaning of the words "capacity" and "ability" but give entirely different viewpoints:

- Maximum current a human can withstand
- Largest hotel in the world

Capacity to withstand maximum current

Electrocution concerns. In the quest to determine the *subtle* differences between *capacity* and *ability*, I became unusually curious about the scientific facts in connection with electrocution and our *capacity* to withstand it. It might have been easy to bypass this subject had it not been for my *innate* concern about the health and well-being of humanity, as seen in my book *The Low Sodium Diet: Stop Agonizing by Embracing a Low Salt Life.*

Also, having experienced the shock of accidently sticking my finger into a plugged-in electric socket taught me a lesson that I occasionally recall. Although I was not hurt since the incident was fleeting, I thought it was worth mentioning. Greater insight into the dangers and prevention of electrocution can be read on the *relevant links* at the end of this chapter.

We're advised that a current of ten milliamperes or 0.01 ampere is sufficient to cause a serious shock that *would* be fatal, and as we advance to a much-higher current level like one hundred milliamperes or 0.1 ampere, contractions of the muscles will start. It is *crucial to note* that since the resistance of our heart is low, a current level as minor as ten milliamperes *can kill us*.

If we're unable to release a handheld tool that causes shocks, the current will be present for a long time; the muscles that control our breathing are not able to move, and our breathing can stop for a period of time. This can occur in the range of thirty milliamperes. Breathing can stop with currents as low as forty-nine volts.

However, this current running through our bodies will never reach the heart because our skin's *capacity* to resist current is far greater and will entirely absorb the current. But if for some reason a *slight current* reaches the heart, *it would be deadly*.

Results of increase in currents

When the current increases to approximately two thousand milliamperes or 0.2 amperes, burns and unconsciousness will occur. Such severity of muscular contraction affects the functioning of the heart. Serious internal burns could then lead to cardiac arrest, and death is possible.

We are not impervious to current

The level of current rushing into our body will depend on how easy it is to be absorbed. Whether the skin is wet or dry is a determining factor in resisting current. Estimation for wet skin is one thousand ohms and greater than five hundred thousand ohms for dry skin. The point of contact is a guideline for measuring resistance.

For example, the internal resistance between the ears is one hundred ohms but about five hundred ohms from finger to toe. Someone with less muscle tissue is prone to be affected at lower current levels. But even in such a case, dangerous injury can happen, depending on the length of time the circuit is exposed to the body. Muscle and fat content variances account for the seriousness of shock that might occur in the body.

For I the Lord thy God will hold thy right
hand, saying unto thee, Fear not; I will help thee.
(Isaiah 41:13 KJV)

As long as we believe the promises of God, we have *an anchor
in the sea of speculation*. After we've exhausted all other sources for
solutions to many of life's complexities, we have the *capacity* to turn
with certainty to the Source that is tried and true. Doing this is a
deterrent to fear, anxiety and is *a rescue* in the face of emergencies.
We can depend on God to keep us peaceful so we don't anticipate
adverse situations.

The following relevant links further substantiate my findings:

Relevant links

www.osha.gov
www.electronics.stackexchange.com
www.sciencebasedlife.com

Hotel Capacity Fun Fact

World's largest located in Malaysia

- First World Hotel & Plaza is the largest in the world. It is located in the Genting Highlands of Malaysia.
- It has set the *Guinness World Records* as being the largest in *capacity*.
- This hotel boasts *7,351* rooms and since its inception in *2006* hosted *35.5 million* guests.
- Although it was dethroned by the Venetian or *Palazzo* in Las Vegas, it later recaptured its title when a new block was opened in *2015*, giving it a much higher *capacity*.

These hotels are so gigantic that they're compared to miniature cities.

Relevant links

www.guinnessworldrecords.com
www.worldatlas.com

Summation of Grammarians

Ability has to be demonstrated, while *capacity* may be described as inborn. How intriguing it is to find out what the differences are between the two words "capacity" and "ability" and *whether they* both mean the same thing! It would be futile for grammarians to undertake the *grueling practice* of examining the meaning of *these words* if the distinctions weren't controversial. Their findings and scrutiny of *etymology* (*the study of the history of words with their original meanings*) are our source.

Using only one of these words

Fascinating scientific conclusions seem to concur that while *both words* may be synonymous, their meanings are not identical. It would be less complicated if we used *only one* of these words without question or compunction.

One definition alludes to *capacity* as "the maximum extent to which an individual is able to receive and retain information," such as in a mental or intellectual *capacity*, or to perform and *endure* tasks such as in physical *capacity*.

A subtle difference

One striking documented phrase refers to the words *capacity* and *ability*: "there's a subtle difference," which clearly implies *there is a difference* between the two words. We know that "similarities are not identities"—things that are similar are not identical.

One of the premises for my research is to have a greater understanding and learning of this topic but *mainly* to show that *with God, our capacities and/abilities can flourish to unknown elevations when we venture out with the energy of our convictions.*

Educators use the term *capacity* in reference to the *perceived abilities*, skills, and expertise of school leaders, teachers, and faculties.

Some clarity with definitions

What an extraordinary opportunity to delve into the truth that *capacity* may be innate while *ability comes from learning and growing.* Knowing where to draw the line can be unnerving. There are distinctions provided to be pondered.

A *prominent* and *beloved* teacher once revealed the truth that if certain words (e.g., body, soul, and spirit) all mean exactly the same thing, then grammar is *devoid as the source of authority* for clarity and the understanding of language. *We'd like to ensure that it's not.*

The following definitions have been taken from several grammatical sources:

- Applied to a person, *ability* and *capacity* mean *about* the same thing but are grammatically different.
- An *ability* to do something, but a *capacity* for doing something
- *Ability* is *qualitative* while *capacity* is *quantitative*
- *Capacity* also refers to a *general ability* to understand a matter or accomplish a task.

Capacity might imply limitation or lack of willingness to reach beyond what can be accomplished. One could also surmise that *capacity* is regarded as having the *potential* to do or participate in something but not the *ability*. So does *capacity imply* limitation?

Capacity: Mental or physical power: e.g.
"You have the power to do better."

125

I did more probing to satisfy my curiosity and desire to compare these two words and noted the following similar meanings:

> Potential: Possible, *as opposed to actual*; capable of being or becoming.
> Latent: Present but not visible, apparent, or actualized; existing as *potential*;
> Dormant: Lying asleep or as if asleep; inactive, as in sleep; *inoperative*; in abeyance
> Abeyance: Temporary inactivity, cessation, or suspension
> (*Psychology*: capacity existing in unconscious or *dormant* form but *potentially* able to achieve expression)

These definitions for *withhold*, in connection with one's *capacity*, are noteworthy: hold back, deny, resist, bridle, suppress, hide, inhibit, reserve.

> Work *Capacity*: perform maximum physical work

Reliable researched definitions confirm that there is a *fine line* between *capacity* and *ability*. What's of interest to me is that *a "line" does exist*.

Relevant links

www.grammaist.com
www.english.stackexchange.com
www.thesaurus.com
www.dictionary.com
www.macmillandictionary.com
www.merriam-webster.com
www.quora.com

An Endnote

The craving of every person is to enjoy a vibrant, abundant life. God's heart for us is even greater. We have the *capacity* to excel as we believe what his Word says about us. We can reach our potentials and realize our aspirations; there's always more inside us than we choose to claim.

We now have a clearer perception of our *capacities* and *abilities!* Many amazing stories of my life and those of family, friends, and acquaintances support the truth that we have the *capacity* to achieve anything we want and that God is not limited by our circumstances or trepidations.

The power lies within us to tap the resources we know are available—the ones we may have been avoiding, not necessarily because of fear but quite possibly because of inhibitions—known only to us. My unconditional desire is to reach as many people as possible with the truth that our adversary, limited in his scope, is evil always, but *God, who is almighty, is good always!*

Hydrangeas: Height Capacities

Fascination and fondness for the *hydrangea plant,* and flowers in general, led me to this chapter. The hydrangea is globally one of the most beautiful flowers that come in massive clusters, ranging in pink, blue, white, and green flowers. With specific names like "mophead," "dwarf," "bombshell," and "snowball," some varieties of this cherished flower are adaptable. They can be trained to grow in various shapes to suit your gardening choice.

Imagine these beauties displayed in over twenty-three species! Many magazines feature them. Most grow to a *capacity* height of fifteen feet. Blooming in late spring, they undoubtedly add sparkle and charm to any garden.

The climbing hydrangea. I recently discovered that the climbing hydrangea reaches *capacity* heights of fifty feet, spreads about six feet, and withstands intense droughts. These boast heart-shaped leaves and white pointed blossoms. As it spreads, it can cover an area of two hundred square feet, providing plentiful shade. This unique variety may take around three to four years to reach the desired height.

Bigleaf hydrangea. Its leaves are enormous, and the maximum height *capacity* is ten feet. Compared to other species, it is the most massively cultivated. Numerous local florists sell them in pots. They're readily available for wedding and church decorations.

Oakleaf hydrangea. It got its name from its foliage, which is like oak leaves and does not tolerate high temperatures as the bigleaf hydrangea. The *capacity* height and width are a maximum of eight feet.

Smooth hydrangea (snowball). These are smaller than others and reach a *capacity* height and width of roughly five feet. The leaves are deep green with a pointed edge. Flowers form encircled white clusters that fade to a light green toward the end of summer. They grow at a steady, rapid pace and don't withstand drought as others do.

Panicle hydrangea. The gorgeous white flowers are tightly compacted. The *capacity* height and width can be as high and wide as fifteen and twelve feet, respectively. This flower withstands cold temperatures in USDA zones 3 through 8. The branches bow down to the earth from the heaviness of the flowers that bloom late in summer.

Bombshell. This flower is a dwarf variety that grows to a *capacity* of three feet tall and four feet wide. Clusters of white flowers can be enjoyed from the middle of summer until fall!

About the Author

Joan Jones is an author and freelance online copywriter, whose professional career began in 2015. Her book *The Low Sodium Diet: Stop Agonizing by Embracing a Low Salt Life* was published in February 2018 and is available on Amazon, where it was on the best-seller list (in its category).

Her dedication to God and family is a lifelong commitment. She enjoys this rewarding life with her husband Phillip and son Kris, who also share her Christian values.

She is a member in good standing with AWAI (American Writers and Artists Institute) and the PWA (The Professional Writers Alliance). She's written several articles and promos that have been published.

Joan worked at the Ohio State University (Health Information Services in Students Health) and the Ohio State Medical Center's Department of Nephrology (medical science that deals with the science of kidney). Within the Department of Nephrology, she assisted in the processing and shipping of biological samples and updated patients concerning their appointments via phone calls. Seeing the behavior and lethargy of kidney patients was her first exposure in recognizing some of the symptoms and effects that the intake of sodium can have on our bodies.

She has volunteered at the Mid-Ohio Foodbank to inspire recipients on how to make healthy food choices. On her websites www. iwriteforhealth.com and www.platterenjoyment.com, she reveals her true passion for caring about matters concerning health and how to live an abundant life!

In her writing, she gleans from experience gained working as administrative assistant and secretary. She has had over twenty years' experience working for corporations like Rockwell International, Cedar Rapids, Iowa; The Coca Cola Company, Atlanta, Georgia; attorneys-at-law firms; and the Pretrial Office, US Federal Courthouse in Columbus, Ohio.

She attended Columbus State Community College.